T0114931

Pearls Of Awareness

Tendai R. Mwanaka

Langaa Research & Publishing CIG
Mankon, Bamenda

Publisher
Langaa RPCIG
Langaa Research & Publishing Common Initiative Group
P.O. Box 902 Mankon
Bamenda
North West Region
Cameroon
Langaagrp@gmail.com
www.langaa-rpcig.net

Distributed in and outside N. America by African Books Collective
orders@africanbookscollective.com
www.africanbookscollective.com

ISBN: 9956-763-88-8

DISCLAIMER
All views expressed in this publication are those of the author and do not
necessarily reflect the views of Langaa RPCIG.

Table of Contents

Acknowledgements

Some of these poems or pieces of have first appeared in the following among other magazines, blogs, anthologies and journals:

Off the Coast, Winning Writers, Kritya, Eleven Eleven, Bruce Poems, Children, churches and daddies and anthologies, Pacific journal Struggle Magazine, Spittoon Magazine, Jenny Magazine, Ginger Piglet Magazine, BLUEPAPER, Deadsnakes, The Blue Hour, Mojoportal, Earthbourne Journal, Calvary cross, Novaim and Napalm, ShotGlass Journal, MelBrake Press, Both Sides Now, Black Magnolis Literary Journal, Poet's stage, Full of Crow, Bursting and Droning mag, The Tower Journal, Fowl Run Press, Exercise Bowler, The Bitchin Kirtsch, Bewildering Stories, Fowl Pox, Decanto, The Phoenix review poetry magazine, Poetrymonthlyinternational, Numinous spiritual magazine, Inclement, Neverbuy poetry, Exiled Ink magazine, Pennine platform, The Red Wheelbarrow, The Delinquent, Neonhighway, Pulsar, New Coin, New Contrast, The Muse- An International Anthology, SCWI journal, ventsalizes.

Section 1: Spiritual

Unbroken Awareness

My life is now a floating shell.
I am a vessel on that river.
The storm, the ship, the sea,
Whose shores we lost in crossing.

I can see the milky distances-
In your eyes, but you cannot see me.
A thin melon slice of first moon,
Melting into songs and slivers of ice.

You could feel small creatures dying.
Cowering humans in their burrows.
Fighting for lives other than theirs.
Aware they could not escape.

Each of us comes into being
Knowing who we are,
What we are supposed to do?
But why do you try to hold back-
The sands, falling in your hourglass?

I am now unconscious.

In a way..., but mute.
A little pearl of awareness,
But this pearl is not me.
Knowing yet unable.

I am now timeless!

All times and in all futures.
I am a universe of windows.
I cannot be touched again.
I am in an endless dream.

But I can see you outlined-
Looking beyond what you know.
One day the seeds would return
And life would continue.

Orientations

We are these cells, this soul, this being.
We are the choices of our own awakening.
We are light that pours through the generations.
Innocent little children dancing to the rain song,
For a season of green to atone for our wrongs.

We are a hunter caught in his own snares.
We are a tidal wave in a sea of broken dreams.
We are flickering whimsy, a breath's laughter.
The sacrificial dove, the hooting owl, the forlorn falcon
O, those surreptitious angels in their sweet anger!
Muttering of dreams lost, deep in our own silences.

We are haunts cries in the aftermaths of battle.
We are fine theatre made out of lost relics.
We are a spider's webs, a tender weave of time.
Over here the wind blows, over there a story told!

We are dry leaves in this intricate whispering.
Augmenting to a morning of silent conversations.
We are this pen conversing to these sentences.
Lighting the threshold to that wordless portent
If we turn, what do we see, a river or a shiver?

Or had we bitten more dreams than we could chew,
And we are now waiting for someone who never comes?

Until You Came To It

There is more of me
I don't know
There is more of you
You don't know
But you are not
To be denied yourself
That you were born
Without knowing
That you were born
Until you came to it.

What Words Would Tell

The sunrise exist in the morning
And the sunset for the evening.

Words vanishing with contact
Perhaps they could be made to exist for
Mornings and evenings of silhouettes.

But what words would tell
The sun to exist for itself?

Water Is My Personal Servant

I saw a river
    Deep in its own chasm
    Turning toward me

Running straight at me
    Cascading through me
    Aware of countless other rivers

I would reveal it to you in words
    If it falls outside your yardsticks
    Then you are dealing with water

The river adapts,
    Causing forgetfulness
    But the water creates

It employs you in awareness
    Stirs your oars
    By the way you think

But every first moon
    Is stealing my water
    I am beginning to hate water

Water is my personal servant
    Through which I have moved
    I can only sense myself in water.

The Choice Is Not Mine.

You can't see
Identifiable landmarks
The cycle lies within me...
I am the sand-river...
Marking time!

My life is an endless river.
Stretching for thousands miles.
My spirit is an ocean without water.
The gap is right here...
Where I have built my myth.

It is not easy to understand me.
Part of the river flows under the sands.
Its only whimsies that brings me out.
I am forced to watch.

I am the ritual.
The centre, the location.
I have honour in you.
Faith in what is said.
Light as that reveals reality.
Summoning one to prayer!

It's mine and mine alone...
The spirit that flows inside me.
It is a river.
Those old, old mysteries...
They are all coming out.
Some patterns do not change.

To hear is to hear
Meaning is whatever speaks.
To see is to see
I will not emerge again.
To be is to be
I cannot evolve again.

Section 2: Inspirational

Intent

Those milky threads of hot energy
cursing through my body.
Weaving stories in the energy
centre of my body.
And I believe my energy centre
is shaped like a circle.
Making me roll through my world.

With my back turned against-
the time of my nearest destination.
For a moment I mistake me-
for a miraculous re-appearance.
As I begin to move towards-
the future.

As the sun says soon,
very soon I will-
rise to shine again.
I want to live it-
all over again.
As if the first time here,
i was just a rehearsal.

Stolen From Death

There was this time when I was
strong.
Full of life, I tried everything
headlong.
When life was rapturously true
Days when I used to rush through,
Life's unending beautiful
adventures.
I remember years ago when we
went.
To lands beyond for daring
ventures.

And it was this other day when I
woke up ill, and so very tired. My
legs couldn't move no matter how
harder I tried to make them do so
and also I couldn't sit on my
haunches. All of my right side was
useless, stricken, like a dried
branch of a tree. I couldn't take
my food with my hands but could
only grovel on my stomach and
guzzle like an old dog. I couldn't
swallow anything hard. I was now
surviving on watery food,
sometimes being spoon-fed like an
infant.

Days when the tragedy befell me,
I used to spend the whole day

crying.
Why had God let these troubles
find me?
Why me? The fury I had, why me?
Against those able to enjoy-
All those enjoyful of life's magic.
Another day I just wanted to die.

It was early in the morning when
my son had gone to the shops to
buy us our food. I didn't want to
be trouble anymore so I took a
razor blade, cut both my wrist's
veins, that I could bleed to death
silently. I don't know how I
managed it and as if by cue my
son returned earlier than I
thought, but I had bled terribly so
bad.

I didn't wish to die anymore, no.
Begging of another go at life again.
That I might enjoy, being lost
moments,
Those are the thoughts that I still
remember,
As my son and friend rushed me.
To the lazer's house that I be
treated,
And be stolen from death like a
leap year.

It was this other day when I woke
up from this sleep and through the
window I could peep at the sun's
lingers filtering everyday, each new
morning, as if there is no end to it
all. I really wanted to live from
that day onwards enjoying every
small and every big moment until
when I would, with satisfaction,
close my eyes for the last time.

A Road To Somewhere

Every whispering path,
Of the forest-
Has to end.

Always follow a single path,
And it will come out-
Somewhere...

I Have Lived Me

What can I possibly see?
In the tracks of my feet.
My body knows it,
What my head denies.
That my spirit dwells inside me
Awakened in my womb
To presence of overwhelming numbers-
answerable to my personal summons.

I have often stopped here
to watch the sun rising
And when the sun lifts over,
It beams gold across grains,
rippling like sand dunes
Sweeping across the land.

And if I turn
I would see the thing
That I could have been.
It came with me
Before I became me,
Recreating me
In my own likeness
For my own ends.

But I am here to dare this.
I would march once more
For I have heroic patience.
I would leave
As I have come,
Without a word.

Hating what I fear
Is a goad to duty?

Section 3: Time & Truth

Time Is Involved In Me

Time is involved in me
In what I would become?

How I Hate It!

I hate it if you going to preach to me, I detest it
because preaching leads to self-fulfilling and
selfish prophecies. Preaching leads to justification
of all sorts of obscenities. Preaching shields evils
behind words and feeds on deliberately twisted
notions and meanings to discredit and distract from
the truth.

I am visiting my rage
Upon this page
No one feels the flames
Commending the organized screams
Of my victims
Ruled by guilt!

Preaching is a privilege and a burden so familiar,
so supportive, and so deadly. Behind every
sermon belies an obscenity and a hypocrite
whose actions are far removed from his words so
I am asking for its removal.

I am a loser
An ultimate alien
Hunting my own wolves
My flesh is good food
Perhaps the predators inside me
Would not prey me?

Are you capable of listening to this story…, or poem?
Is it a poem as such, and do you have the ears to hear?
On your head, I mean here and there. I will repeat it,

and by repetition, I impress upon the lessons and perhaps
it would be made to go!

You don't get the unexpected
Small animals sometimes emerges
Questioning your whims and moods
With minds that smells your bleeding sighs
But can't we have some little light?
It could really be employed here

The first missionaries of the Catholic Church spread this
disease and salvaging a complete uniform is no longer
possible because they can only groan silently in their graves.
I suppose they wanted to cross all those unidentifiable
landmarks of their sermons with their words. You can also cry
out with them, and that's the tone I have always wanted to
set with you.

IF I LIE

If I lie...
Then I do not know
It has a ring of the truth.

Nobody Tells The Truth

When a thing vanishes
And then-
Suddenly comes back
Nobody tells
The truth
Even when everyone knows
The shapes
In the shadows

And a cult of
Personal honesty
Leaves not shadows
But hidden shells
Within hidden shells
Of all the things
That we had felt
As the truth
All going away.

See How It Begins To Distort

Guard every speech
That you say

Because it carries
The warmth and moistures
Of your life

See how this utterance
Begins to distort
Everything

It is a seeker
Of sensations
Knowledge is...

Just a side effect
Residing
In these particulars

Too Far From Your Time

I could have made you feel-
   inadequate.
And I cannot ask you-
   to forgive me.

But that you could try-
   to understand.
Too far-
   from your time.

Section 4: Life & Memories

Grains Of Insight

There is a separate
     Violent intimacy
     In the wind trawling the clouds
Like a pure jazz of form.

The pours of January rains
     And the sloping drops of rain
     Accumulating melancholies
Hungry and white as salt.

The rains won't stop its jazz
     Balanced in the oval of heaven.
     Dynamic thoughts glimpsed
In the lines of the rain.

Needing a certain guide
     To really see the yield.
     As the years accumulate
The grains of insight.

Mind and eye composing
     Thoughts straight, sometimes
     Circular, diagonal, oblique.
But the outlines are still visible.

Thoughts this transformed
     Informs this pilgrim
     Like you.

Maybe unlike you!

Listen To Your Anger

The landscapes we have passed.
        Galaxies implanted upon us.
Rules changing with every surprise.
        Connections being broken and...
The knowledge that we are a mote.
        We have seen them all...

You have cried out yourself.
        You have suffered wounds.
You have felt them all.
        But something is still revolving.
You are still human.
        But sometimes time runs out.
For you and me

We must do what we must.
        Others have survived us.
You did, they did! I did!
        We will be there someday.
Only this matters.
        Our soul suffices this night.

Don't listen to it.
        Listen to your anger and rage.
And stand on the battlegrounds.
        You do not need to take witnesses.

We have cluttered this life.
        Anger is a clutter, hate, rage...
Everything is locks, closures, doors...
        We are blind participants dancing-

To the songs we do not hear.
       The performers suited to the designs.

On A Summer Herding Day

Early morning it is and Bhoyidho,
My brother, all the boys and me

Of our village.

Wake up early to eat, for-
  This lovely day ahead of us.
    For very soon the sun will rise-
      Over the dawn blue Mozi mountain.

With the sun smiling its sweet,
Lovely smile, oh so lovely!

So is us!

Moo, hey, Jamaica ahoy to a new day.
  We took our sheep and cattle,
    Goats, sheep, dogs, food and all.
      Aha! We will have a good day.

Birds singing sweetly from the trees.
The cuckoo bird cooing us forward-

To the grazing lands.

Cuckoo-roo, cuckoo-roo, cuckoroo-wee.
  To so abundant with reeds a veldt.
    Green grass, water and fruits
      We will spend the day there, never worry.

Of Matron and her troop of troublesome-

Bromley, Venekadanga and Nhengamuswe.

The fields are far!

We never will about them, nor the sun.
  Its early in the morning, the sun is still so young.
    We will play; we will have a long day.
      Brawl, hunt and play soccer.

Now, my brother and other older boys-
Divide us into twos for the first-

Calling of the day.

I am with Solomon, that it always is like.
  Whoever will loose the fight would while,
    The whole day doing the other's daily duty when-
      In the sun like a king the other basks.

Its only yesterday that I had spent the day
Looking after the cattle, not today, no!

I have to win.

He has piercingly fierce jibs.
  And could pack them in thousands.
    But I have power to shove and send-
      Him down to the ground, making it easy.

I will rejoice if he falls down,
I will sit on top of his stomach.

That's his end!

I will pounce his face like a hammer-
  Striking with no mercy on the nail's head.
    Until he surrenders to me-
      His king who will rule him today.

Near midday as the sun builds-
Pouncing the veldt with fierce heat,

We start hunting!

Chasing guinea fowl, till they are-
  Tired and start running on legs.
    And that's easily when our dogs-
      Will snatch them after a short run.

We will chase and catch wild hare,
Doe, deer, fawn, locust and share-

Even monkeys?

Which we train to be our good friends.
  But as the sun starts staring the eastern hem,
    We engage into wild frenzy.
      Into two groups we engage in soccer.

As the sun touches the western mountains-
Sitting on top of them as if taking its-

Last look at us.

Then we start searching, rounding, fully.
  Strayed and lost cattle to one spot.
    When we have them together we trace.

Our footsteps back home joyfully.

Days when we have failed to track,
The strayed Matron and her troop,

They are home already.

Bromley has led them back home.
  All the way to our fields, eating not.
    A crop from other people's fields, no.
      We wait for, we know, a heavy thrashing.

When everyone is cosy around the fire-
And those waiting for their cattle are fed.

We arrive home.

Some will scold and shout at us for,
  Always being late with their cattle.
    At such instances we don't give voice to-
      The bad vibes we want to say to them.

When every cattle has been located,
And all owners have gone with their lot,

Without a loss.

We go home rejoicing of a good day.
  And when we have the cattle securely shut.
    We proceed home with our day's show.
      Father forgets to beat us sometimes.

What, with all the meat we have brought-
Sweet roasting and the smells of meat.

We all feast!

Mother and Father, our sisters, gratefully-
  Listening to stories that we tell of the day.
   And laughing heart fully, we all did-
     Happily as we surrounded the grate.

Messages of a Forefinger

I have always been quicker
Except when I was slower
I have always had both
But the test always comes first
On a way to a splintered person
It is only a whim
That can be able to stop me

I am spurring for time
So I would accept everything
Thus I accept nothing
And I accept them, merely
The messages of a forefinger
As it once was..., a surprise
Of all the things that I hadn't known
Visited upon this page

The sanctuary of the past
Is an attitude-object lesson?
Cancelled underneath a carpet of regrets
That, at least
Has not changed much
The genie is still alive
The past as fog between the trees

O Ocean

What would be an ocean?
Without cloudless
Blue skies.

For perfection
Is a machine fantasy?
And fantasies
Of the conjurer.

I Remember

I remember I was a child once-
Some years ago I loved one.
Year, times I have been happy.
I remember, weren't there sweet little
Tappy, a friend, I dearly remember.

When I look back to those years,
I remember the cheerful old ways.
By break of dawn we were at the river.
So chilly and cold we all shiver.
I remember how serene and silver-
The river was as we fetched water.

The sun brightly shinning over Mozi Mountains.
Spreading his sparkling warm fingers.
Over lush green hills and valleys, lingering-
Bright blue mist sneaking from picturesque banks.
We could hear the birds singing from the sky.
A sweet lovely song from so far away.
Was it a song of a young man in love?

I remember sitting under our Mususu tree.
A tree as old as grandma Helen.
So immortal like the rock of ages.
Eating from Grandma's black clay pots.
Pumpkins, yams, sweet potatoes and nuts.
I remember my sister, a garrulous glutton.
Gire, do you remember that tonnage,
Of sweet eatings, aha I want to laugh-

At how you used to brood over everything.
Like mother hen over her little things.
Jealous of any hands, eyes and mouths-
Directed at your tonne of those full mouths.
I remember me and my brother Bernard-
Gourmands were these two little brats.
Aha, so sweet and funny were the times.

I remember playing in dusty fields and paths.
A game of soccer during late winter days.
Rhaka-rakha, fish-fish, bottle dunhu, till dusk.
Never thinking of anything but play.
And like angels in paradise, who was a girl?
All equal, boys and girls enjoying gaily.
Until we were hot and naughty from play.

We all swarm like bees for the river.
All that shrieking, giggling, splattering-
Water flown so far into the sky-high.
I remember playing "Chitsvare" in Nyajezi.
At deep sage green "Tanganda" pool.
Ask our fathers they swarm there past.
I remember diving from high above-
Into the cool sweet waters of Tanganda.

Was it
buttered pumpkin leaves and "Sadza"?
goat's meat, fresh vegetables and Sadza?
"Rupiza" or "Mutakura" from cowpeas?
I remember eating delicious and tasty meals.
Our stomachs bulging tightly and shiny, like honey-
We washed down with sweet sour "Mahewu".
Cupfuls of sweet sour down our throats.

"Hwai, hwai huyai", merry sweet little voices were-
  calling on young innocent sheep that we were.
"Tinotya", what do they fear so clear a night?
A full moon wonderfully probing and bright.
Like distant campfires, stars sparkling untired.
  "Mhomhi", they are all gone to "Mutare".
    The wolves will never come back, not for us.
    Do come please, "Chiuyai henyu".

    Trudging, treading, O, to thunder of flying legs, hello!
    Bumping against one another, a tiny blot of humanity.
  Here we come, fast, deftly and cleverly.
Oh thin air here! Aha Josephina is caught.
  Until left only was Enia, our revered cat.
    But no, she can't go past us.
    Yet those times have gone past.

    We change fastly, notice, we never!
    Swept along the tide like waters in the river.
  With nostalgia we admire youths rover.
  What if we could go back, we all ponder?
Do the waters in Nyajezi go back, up the terrain?
  Like dark flooding waters, big trunk trees and stones-
    They make new pools, ravines, beaches and courses.
    These scars we have are notices of changes and times-
Roads, paths and places we have gone through.

If We Only Keep To It

Unconscious things,
           have to run-
                 their natural courses.

The moon frosted horizons-
           knew the things,
                 which were emerging.

Beginnings of intense loyalty,
           travelling companions-
                 have of the other.

This is as good-
           a direction as any other,
                 if we can only keep to it.

It's only the wind that lives alone,
           and we can only drink this wind.
                 For we are dead if separate.

Old And New

The sun above the horizon-
Is painting golden lines.

Of old and new...
And places in between.

Section 5: Death, Loss & Loneliness

Child To Child

The time ahead of them
Was of little choice

A thing passed from child
To child to child

To Agony of Death

Constantly being aware
Of the consequences of
Our beings, the souls
Of my people.

And creatures
Of that old cold hunt
Lost and concealed
Lessons lost too.

The first thirst of
Desperation
Is a moat of agony?
That disturbs the mind
It is a thirst
At the edges of the sea

And all time chimes
To this call
Impaled on a thorn of
Chance or something
To experience for itself.

Grandmother's Bones

I returned to my grandmother's grave
  We were burying an old uncle
    And it started raining

So I hid under Mususu tree
  Near my grandmother's grave
    It is not the grave
      She is buried in

The rain kept coming down
  I stayed behind, alone
    And as the rain got the leaves
      And drench me

I felt the smell
  Of her old bones
    Coming out of the grave
      And I ran away and ran
        And I am still running today

To The Wind

The wind has a silver look.
   The wind is surgeon's knife cutting away its
own skin
      to expose what's underneath its waves.

In a cluster of mud-hovels just beyond my
tracks I saw a sudden opening
of things that were once concealed.

     And I saw as much as I was capable of.
   Surprise shocking myself alive,
sacrifice and agony making me feel stronger.

My body like plantings of poverty grass
that is at the ragged edges of that broken
opening.

And the setting sun floating low a faded dim
orange by the recent storm.
   Rain still crouching lower in those clouds
     and the wind piling up those clouds
together.

Sensing this filtering of things to hear other
sounds
at the flinty borderlines of those darkening
diameters.
Sounds tumbling like small raindrops from
those clouds to become thin water cover...,
turning the soil into its own limits.

The drenching wash of death, desire
and doubts are bathetic mothers of vagaries
        that never really drench me.
    They are like a ghost rain, a downpour that
never touches those clouds
and the ground.

My thoughts like a compass arrow
but my body is but an echo of what I used to
be.
One could see me clearly.
I must be the wind today,
steady wind collecting the leaves.

Norman

When I am lonely
"Norman"

You stare your image into my
Reflections

And go right into my hidden
Tears

Maybe you were only gazing at
My beauty

But also making certain that
I exist

In This Sea

I would swim in the cup of this moon.
An ambient sea imaging around me.
Toll sighs clinging to my darkling skin.
The white-wind neighing above this sea.

Returning to haunt me again and again.
The luminous flames of my distant past.
"No!" They would never leave me alone.
I listened to the soothing voice within them.

The bell of a wandering cow in winter,
Like the moaning toll of a furrowing plough.
And it told me only this long story,
I am the sound and only soul in this sea.

I Am The Only Needle

I am the only needle
In my name and of my calling.
Impossible needle stabbing the sky.
And there is no other needle
Of any kind anywhere.
Which can call upon me
For anything.

Not even for the sewing
Of the tattered clothing.
Not even for compromise
Or for cohabitation.
Not even for the slightest begging
Of an agreement
Or any arrangement.

I Have Achieved Me

The palimpsest bliss is the green-
glimmer of the sun corona.
  People in huge..., terribly huge
numbers as they dip into shadows
    and their meanings are lost.

  The colours of those distant rocks:
        grey, gold...deep amber!
  A line of brown grey, pale-pasted
        ribbons of rocks
are like hues of an egret's feathers...,
        flying past me, the past:
  It is like rocks flying on their own
        fingers.

The faint sound of voices fixing into
my memories
  and bestowing the inward view to give
myself a little rope
    to haul inwards.
    I know it, I have always known it:
        that something is broken inside
me.

      It is an ancient conceit
to think that there is only one sound in
        this entire universe
  and everything else is just echoes of
        that sound.
But I will tunnel in like victims always
        surviving this abuse

by speaking to fish in my own dreams
without even the need to respond to
myself.

There is nothing I can do now but
don't ever think
  that I am a coward, for once I was in
love,
    and I loved her so much more...that
wild, wild shore.
      And now I am thankful that I have
achieved me.

For you are studying me intimately and
    I am in these tamed records
  You only have a face to measure me
          by.

But don't sheath your blade; draw the
blood of a finger
  and create your own river.
    Who owns this river passage?
      Not you, none of us, no one is...
        More transparent than these
muddied waters
          that are the blood waters of our
fingers.

Section 6: Freedom & Political

Myth Killers

A party is a shared dream
The army, the man-machine
Created our present dream.
Myth dies when a party dies
This is the dream we share
We are myth-killers!

A ring of strange thought
To be thought of as a god
Can become an anathema.
And the hoards within laughs
From their inward arena.
Damn those little Pharaohs!
They are the last of that lot.

Arriving at the dusk line
This is the shock
To find yourself alive.
My name, I know my name
And here I am
Hidden behind my name.

Like a malleable infant
I am conditioned to kill
Its in my guts.
Like esters of a perfume
Telling me to look beyond
Paradoxes in these dry dreams.

What Are You Waiting For

Interpretation of the poem, ORIENTATIONS

We are these cells
This soul, this being
We are the children's bones
Which you now chew
With lips of a sunset.

We are the choices
The reasons
Of our own awakening.

We are light
That has sipped
Through the windows
For all these generations.

Innocent little children
Dancing to Mugabe's songs
For a season of enough food
To atone for his angers.

We are a hunter
Prowling, punting, caught
In his own snares
That the hunter could
Would…, did dream!

We are a tidal wave
In Limpopo river
Of desiccated corpses
And broken dreams

Going somewhere?

We are flickering whimsy
The world's laughter
And like playground tricks,
Limpopo's breezes
Is just a breath's laughter.

We are the sacrificial dove
The hooting owl
The forlorn falcon!
O those surreptitious angels
In their sweet anger
Sour anger, so angry.

Muttering of dreams
Deep, dreams deep, lost
In our own silences.

We are haunts cries
Zimbabwe 's little children
Maimed, touched, butchered
The aftermaths of, wrecks of
The world's silent battles.

We are Mugabe's little
Lilies, roses, vegetable-
Garden, a fine theatre
Of lost relics, so damned
See, just look at this beauty
Built upon your rejections.

For the sun is rising

In the favoured east
The west is now busy
In its own illusoriness
Gazing at this spider
Weaving allowed webs.

And that angry tinder
Has become this desperate
Time's warped old man
Weaving, always weaving
Echoes of his own angry youth
Tender weaves of a time.

Over there in Masvingo
Over there in Manicaland
The winds of change is blowing
Over there in Harare
Over there in Bulawayo
A story has been told.

What else do you want
To hear for you to believe
The cries you have heard
Stop this man, please stop him
For we don't need him anymore.

Where is the UN
Where are you USA, UK
Europe , Australia , Canada
China doesn't give a hoot
But for our mines, factories, labour
And the east is in silent approval
Thabo is Mugabe's little terrier

Africa has thanked us with.

And we are now dry leaves
In their intricate whisperings
Being blown here and there
With no place of our own
Refugees in our birthright
The world's sight of contempt.

Augmenting to a morning
Afternoon and night
Year after year, and another
Of their silent conversations
Known as silent diplomacy.

Always quivering to Mugabe's trickery
And lying to an uncaring world
Hear that fool, just listen to his
"We are engaged in silent…
diplomacy, silent diplomacy my foot!
My life! Bugger off old crooks.

"There is no African problem"
Smith and Muzorewa smothered
Newsman with Kipling's genius
Yet Zimbabwe is still a boiling pot
Making garbage soups
And Mugabe's blood cocktails
Whilst Mbeki smothers
The world with Mugabe's refrain
"THERE IS NO CRISSIS IN ZIMBABWE."

We are this pen

These resistances, the unappreciated
Voters whose vote is stolen in daylight.

We are the aftermaths of voting
Casualties, casualties, casualties
Constructing these sentences
All alone, unaided, lighting
The threshold to that wordless potent.

Rise up, O rise up!
Our beloved country men
Wise up, O wise up!
The silences beyond our borders
Do you want another
Rwanda , Kenya , Burundi...

Turn your eyes
From the riches of oil
O the oil, if we had oil
Rather than blood in our rivers
Just think of...

That child in Murehwa
That young man in Nyanga
That old woman in Zaka east
And that tot in Mazowe east
They have been striped naked.

Look at that child-
What do you see?
Have you seen the rivers?
Of tears, blood and sweat
All over her body.

Have we believed too much
In Africa, UN, and the USA
Australia , Canada and EU
Or have we bitten more dreams
Than Mbeki could ever chew
And we are now waiting
For someone who never comes.

Only one path remains son of the soil
Through the harsh and arid desert
To where love and hope
Refuses to its unrefusing core
O, why, what are you waiting for?

I Have A Legacy

I *am not a leader*
 because I do not take responsibility
of my own actions

I *am not a guide*
 because I do not warn them with words,
  words are often useless.

I *am not God, not even a god,*
 but maybe a demiurge
  who sometimes basks in my own godhood.

I *wish I had never occurred*
 inside their own sun.
  Some other times…,

I *am not fully human*
 but humans
  have just been as cruel.

I *am not insane*
 but I am insensitive
  to the use of power.

I *am not a tyrant*
 but I have been cruel
  on so many occasions.

I *am so closer yet so far*
 to what I should be,
  but I have a legacy.

They would be very keen to understand me,
and will frame me in their own words…,
they would seek the truth.
Yes, it is possible to understand me
but what they have always done with it
has always been another thing.
I have a spirit world emerging into the open spaces.
My spirit dwells outside walls answerable to no one,
not even to me, but to dimensions of closed things
and I have trained my eyes to estimate these dimensions.
I often have stopped here to survey the scenes
in my teapot-shaped playing ground.
Faces looked unto me…
Faces and faces and faces.
For I am their delegate and
I would give them my death waters.
All the numerous tribes and they shall consecrate it
to an unknown spirit and that spirit used to be me
before I became like another Amin.
I am their silent forced unity and
  they would never question my decisions.
    They would only act.
      Personal danger will not deter them
       They would serve me.
They are my people, keepers of my faith
I would they would live forever.
Their lives would never cross dry paths.
I am a singular movement which they mistake for a dictator.
  I am not a dictator. No! But
    I am consciousness lost to memory.
      And they would carry the mysteries of me throughout their lives.
I would always be present in their lives,
shading responses

They would sense a physical presence…,
memories of me speaking to their senses.

I am a building of many-
  many windows,
    whatever are the window frames but-

I can't see the thing
  that is inside this building
    for my windows do not allow me.

I am a dust of their mistreatments.
Me and my people for all these centuries.

I am now the talisman of their lives
even though some of my people still think-

I am the ancient norm against which
the new must be measured.

I am meals in a cave
  crowded by little demons and gods,
    but don't feel bound to try-
      odours of this ancient decay.

Education always take time
The new one would take time too
but it is not measurable.
It is eons and eons of necessities.
But like a cyclical pattern the new one is already lost to them.
And that copy they are holding onto is worse than having nothing
The change is always non change.

Bad Vibes

Vibes, bad vibes, good vibes.
Black, black vibes, black wrongs.
Colonialism, injustices, guilty.
The disputes, the disappointments,
The death certificate says it all.
So much fodder for the hate makers.
Go good people,
Have yourselves a ball!

Black, black vibes, dirty.
Tainted, ruffian, prohibited.
Stamped feet, curses, and prayers.
Wheedling, cajoling, bargaining.
The sun laughs at this quota,
And some live lives harder than others.

Black, black magic, funerals.
Offender, backward, an unborn route.
Broken teeth, smashed dreams,
So passionate, all consuming, hurtful.
We are immersed in the minutes,
Of invisible wounds bleeding.
The inwardness of a candle,
Is just a mere breath?

Black, black vibes, good vibes.
Angry, temperaments, threats.
Orgiastic, forgiving, and healing.
Laughter is like the Rhine's algebra.
Sets the stage for the next cycle.
Time can also be a place-
Wed me please, a shapelier dream.

Seeds of Ruin

A curtain of iron is
A stone that excludes.
It is an aristocrat of the sword.
And like survival patterns-
Privilege creates arrogance
And arrogance promotes injustice.

And they would not believe it
  That what lies beyond
    Is more important
      Than now, or even
        What lies behind?

This is the choice they made
For, and by themselves.
And you have to discover it for them,
and for yourself.
Come right up against it.
Let your anger shout it.

How like a little boy he is...,
  The oldest man of our universe.
    Yet the youngest!
      Both in one flesh
        The seeds of ruin blossoms.

Waiting Still

A song that can sing songs
Of that olden trek

It is like a seed of the past
Waiting for me.

And a little wind has covered
All our tracks.

But I still have this
Soft burning.

And I am kept alive by it
Waiting still.

It Is Not Moved By Me

Bass strings like rain drumming
Underneath a whisper of middle strings
Is like a cry of the caged

The Bali set is like an autumn wind
It is like a memory of freedom

Was it always like these strings
That freedom requires rebellion

But like lute-player's fingers
Light changes on its own patterns
It is not moved by me.

"Go!"

An unmistakable cry for it is the quite murmur. One word containing countless messages of life and conversations of death. A deep condor, so draining! Those internecine mass killing fields are the ravages of Mugabe's Zanuphobia and those flights into xenophobia; Intrigue, migrations, deportations.

Leg-arching and lung-arching runs through Mbeki's dishevelled nights. But his face blinks and his eyes winks Even my father is not content but lives so uncomfortably for he cannot touch himself in my memories. And I can sympathies with him for failure is its own demonstration. But his shadow must learn to share the fears and consequences of how many more of me he is always willing to replace, always raging against every adjacent difference.

The memories have slowed him down and I have picked up pace cursing backwards into the ocean- slowly, step by step, I said slowly.

And I hunt specific fish, all of them are mine and I said all of them are mine..., small star-flower blossoms, tiny like deep water vectors. And I scoop them in my arms..., I said all of them into my arms.

Johannesburg

A town on the far
away clouds, low-slanted
Light of the south.

And the glow of this town
is like a window into my past.

But I am now a part
of this town.

Rejecting
only the waters in those
drifting clouds.

Our Desert Of Our Desert

The blowing wind
Is like a fog
Obscuring our rising sun
And this is the desert
The desert of our desert

And distant people
Are always our enemies?
Unless they throw
Sand into the air

For the hand
That throws the sand
Does not hold a sword

And this is where
We were born
And we permit ourselves
To know nothing else

To Seed and Grow Stronger

The inner faces of sheer rivers
That I could not see-
Waters of their depths

But I know
The water is there
The earth knows it too

They would be night birds
Drawing damp shadows
Across the water

And on the embankment
Are creatures that lives on sunlight
In another world.

And if I put my ear
The earth speaks
With sounds of distant rapids

And when I dip to drink
They are ripples
Which the river takes away.

Even at this distance
I feel the rapids
Of the far away waters

Like something unrelenting
From my past
Disappearing inside me.

The rivers searches
To drink up raw earth
To seed and grow stronger.

Remnants

I was born the year the locust drifted
northwards
like darkling clouds of my inescapable
memories.
And I am the source of their survival
for the locust
had eaten everything.

My life is an illusive fragrant like
voices of the waterfalls,
I drifted into this presence this
morning.
I don't like answers, voices, other
names, other places,
and questions in all my answers.
And I can see little else but myself.

Yesterday I was something else and
tomorrow,
what would I become?
I have not chosen this map that is
sending me to the north
whilst everyone else is drifting
southwards.

I can't delay you to help me escape
and
I can't deny you such experiences, but
I can feel the price you have paid.

And you will..., someday-

Understand that I am content even
though you think
that I am a coward.
How so little you know of me!

But all that I am don't matter now for
my waters are drying
and it's the odour that's left.
Do you think I don't feel this: that
failure is my persona?

But it's my power that I tell us and it's
my gift
that I peer now and again through the
veil of time.
It's my power that I tell us the
meaninglessness
and pitfalls of our human nature.

I am one of yours and I know that
you have not given up
the belief that you and you alone...
Hold the key!
And I am like you!

A little more like remnants but
whatever I would be-
My fire must have its damper and the
rubble would have the rest.

I Cannot See You

What adventures have we experienced
from animal furs to human garments?
What hardships of our youths
are the long steps of our ladder?

We would make another long leap,
but we need water rings
because this room would reject us.
I mean here..., this time.
Testing us...,
this time is always testing us.

Too much has happened, too much...I
said too much has happened to us and
there is no honest reality anymore.
And if you don't trust me, then I must
pity you for trust is my first reality.

It is the designs of my religion, wheels
and wheels upon wheels, rolling...
Rolling like an insane wheel.
Even these will go...,

You are looking for another frontier?
We could go there and never return,
really! We will grow, we will evolve.
Are there any strange animals where
you are going?

Find it in your palms, this planet for
you are holding it..., find it!

You anger knows it where your reason
does not.

Cling to it!
Wallow in it!

How does a child know it and what
would a child choose? Your youth still
demands that you be given your
moment.

But if one of us dies...It is only the
required event
for one direction is as good as
another.
We cannot go back...

The sun comes up; Sand is soft
beneath our feet and this is what we
drink. The sand is our enemy. The
longer we endure it the more
vulnerable we are.

I love you by right of loneliness and I
read you by your emotions.
This is the worth of your measure-
The motivation for the leap is lost in
this revelation.

My love does not discard, accumulate,
stimulate, delude...My love is without centre,
self... My love has no desires of results, goals,
perfections, visions... My love accepts your

nakedness.

You say you are not arguing, but that I
    permit you to know nothing else.
     This derives from our ancestors.
      For we can create nothing, but
            ourselves.

We can see our tracks on the sands,
but our tracks do not have flesh. You
will go..., but may never return and I
cannot follow you.
Because I cannot see you.

The Sun Exists In Itself

I take up my subject and let it
be..., about religion, and they
say, is he capable? Then my
mouth opens up awareness,
cursing backwards to a time
lost in mystery, a time without
parallels, invoking the licence
to dream! Peering
down...down...down, I see
people with layers, free-verse
eyes in their faces and I feel so
lonely, I cannot pray. Praying
like prayer is a demand for pity
in the power of desperation.
Like giving death-waters to
death. Religions like
individuals wreck from within
and some live lives like
mayflies. I can see their ending
in ice but not soon enough as
I endure it. How I hate ice: My
body frozen! I want you to
look into this horror...That
you are seeing now, without
seeing it or knowing it and if I
could, I would shed tears and
consider this wish as an act.
This wish would become a
miracle and you are as great as
any miracle that you can think
of because you speak with

your own life. Speaking directly into your senses, speaking things not cast in words because you do not need words. *And if I choose good does that make you bad and if you choose bad...Does that make me good? Must we always judge: Must we always seek forgiveness? The sun exists in itself!* When you behold a rainbow what colour do you like most? Do you think all the other colours would die for want of the colour that you have chosen? Dying like when a thing vanishes and leaves no shadows! But I can see their shadows and I can see them walking silently and I can feel...The sour colours of their fears driving inside me like hungry pains, like minutiae of an angry humanity. Hungry for lost infinity! But we still carry the detritus with us because we did not separate, scatter out at night, this night-
Or another; Time did not stop for us. We had the choice everyone has: *To die now or to die later... Now live where the fear of being...and the love of being reside in rooms next to each other. Now*

live where the courage of love...and the faith in life resides in a time that changes the past. Now live for the quality of activity. For you are a seed blown in yesterday's winds and you would be tomorrow's plume tree. Where the nightingale nestles its cares, its feathers, its eggs. And I feel the satellites of my life. Instruments which plays music; warming, cooling, addressing. My fears, my angers, my memories. Memories of myself uncovering the holy city that I see in distances. So beautiful in the morning light! And I was like that city once but it was in another life. In another lifetime..., a lifetime that does not have ties with any time. A lifetime that dissolves with contact!

A Poet's Mimesis:

Magnification

I was a small bit of blood in my
mother's heart and womb. I was not
larger than a cherry plum but look at
me now. I was born a poem.

Perpetual genesis

I can form a composite of genetic
suggestions of me.
I can form a new kind of mimesis…,
I can form a poet's something else
sloughing away from me…,
which could have been something.
I can form a sum of all the things that
I might have been.

Biological invention

Only faint vague shapes, which were
once human remain on this collapsed
foaming greyness. A bit of red
streaked bone, bones holding the
form of checks and brows. Very poor
material to shape a new poem!

The sun of understanding

I am the middle of my own poem
looking inwards because I know

where it is that I live
I am the middle of my own poem
looking in ways no inner eye,
no inner voice cannot see and cannot
say.
I am the middle of my own poem
looking in ways I cannot share.

Now I am this

The only thing that I truly understand
is that I know who I am and what I
was, for once I was a child..., and now
I am this. And all the rest has been
lost in shadows of memories, hidden,
all gone away.

I believe

There is no ceiling over me but only
an open sky so full of changes.
And my moistures are channelled into
this sky.
This sky is now an opposing
synchrony that threatens me with
turmoil

I am a mirror image

But the outlines of me are still there
because I have always diverged. I have
never had concurrent points but
echoes of bones and joints.

See my shapes, see my curves, see my insides. I am shinning through your eyes.

My Mortal immortality

I have denied myself form so that I
would remain formless,
hiding but not finding myself.
My life is now dominated by mystical
caprices-
that relentlessly consigns me to a
speculative realm.

The scattering

But I still have a connection here if I
can only find my scattered bits before
others have found them.
But I would let them scatter, run and
hide anywhere. Even in a poem of
their choice.

The choices

Let them, but I did not let them,
because I know that they would carry
with them the seeds of their own
survival.
that would make it impossible for me
to find their centre:
"Not to forgive."
And I am always fighting against this

tide:
"Never to forgive."

The time of the stomach

In the time of the stomach the words
of my own poem precipitates into
crises unanticipated. Maybe that's
always the way it should be. But I
always carry with me water when I
leave the universe of my poem
because out there, there are just some
few dewdrops hanging on damp
Acacia leaves. Each always a promise
of pain!

Destiny

To the east, waits Nyanga Mountain
and to the west there is Nyangombe
River.
But one foot ahead of another I have
always moved as I have.
Not trying to match anyone because I
have my own destination.

Perseverance

A plodding perseverance would
deliver me. Thus I would create my
own supernatural and sensing it at
every turn by the sheer power of my
own will.

I am a poem

I am a poem, a slanting shadow, a thin
rope,
a crumbling bulge!
I am a poem, a tiny lip of rock..., here
And another over there...there.

And when this poem is not long
enough then it is not long enough and
any other way of thinking is not as
long as this poem is long.

Climbing the mountain

I am a particle defying gravity, a
finger-hold here..., a toehold there...,
clinging to the rock surface. I have
known what it is to be a poem with
various, momentous meanings. Look
at me now!

The world of no birds

In a world without birds I have always
invented my own poem-
to link one piece of time to another
and when I have passed,
I would never be the same poem
again.

The world of birds

In a world of birds everything that I
am drops into a no sound, and I have
created a common catastrophe that
binds the decorations of my poem
together.

Decorations?

Decorations, are how we prepare for
our own sacrifices.
Decorations, are how we refuse to
reject,
and regret for what cannot be.

They are the decorations in all the
poet's poems,
and all their imitations but they fail to
stitch together the essences of a
tomorrow. And all our inventions fail
to fuel this tomorrow's diesel engines.

I was born a poem

But life has made me whole yet I was
born a poem-
like a mirror of my own life striking a
river.
I would never die the way I came,
Plunging into the mystical and dreams
of termination, no!

I was born poetical

And between the usual poem and the
unusual poem there is very little space
for my own poem to be immortal.
And it is always poetical to thank
yourself for this little space.

My dream, the collective I

A dream inhabited by glimpses of
silver-edged things in water-
shimmering in their greying colours
like trout,
Igniting an ancient memory of silver-
flesh dazzling my appetite,
in a banquets of the uninitiated
hungry.

My soul

A spangle of shattered flesh
attempting a butterfly design; my soul,
my poem... Digesting its own
experiences. Not answers, not
questions, for it is time for
conjectures.

The language of If

If I had only...
It is only fools who prefer living in the
past or even the present

If we can only...
Immerse ourselves among these fools,
their past and this present.
In a time of pure alternation.

The present and the past

Unless if you are trapped you can't
built your future out of your present...,
a present which does not even exist?
But as if it were, rows on rows of eyes
with senses lost, like eyes of a gasping
fish squirming in pain. It is a future
furrowed in this present and the past.

I was there

I know-
I was there..., at the instant that has
left you.
I want to assure you that it is forever
out of your reach.
And that there is no substitute of this
instant and time,
Time as an alienating device!

There is no time

There is no time..., just a little bit of
time to shape the edges of the weather
which always have square meanings
that stoutly refuses arrangement.

The patterns

These patterns, this poem in my mind,
conducting the waves downwind.
And the wind of the south hungering
for empty spaces.
The wind's fingers sifting through the
clouds...,
driving dark clouds toward me.

Judgement day

That the cloud-darkness of holly
judgement might appear? Silence
threatening hearing, and anything...
And everything else is possible. For it
is not silent in my mind and nothing
tells you apart from me. If you were
me you would run too.